This is a welcome col [illegible] short prayers in what many see as a frightfully busy world. We are reminded that there is always room for prayer despite our busyness. These succinct and incisive prayers help to counter the pressures of modern life, of intrusive technology, and widespread commercialism. The book *Life's Complicated: Pray Simply* guides us back to a still, listening and loving God.

The Reverend Canon Dr Mark Dimond

Human, heartfelt, concise, simple and tender prayers; clearly rooted in the God of love who is in Christ. At the end of our day, the only thing that matters is prayer, and it is clear from *Life's Complicated: Pray Simply* that prayer matters to the Reverend Andrew Highway.

The Right Reverend David Wilbourne

About the Author

The Reverend Andrew Highway is an Anglican Priest with the Diocese of Llandaff, the Church in Wales. He grew up in the city of Coventry and then the market town of Chipping Sodbury in South Gloucestershire on the edge of the Cotswolds, and is the son of a Baptist minister. Andrew studied at Saint Michael's Theological College, United Kingdom, and was ordained by the Archbishop of Wales at Llandaff Cathedral in 2012. As a non-stipendiary minister, Andrew works as a Town Centre Manager in Local Government. In his vocational capacity, Andrew serves as a Priest in parish ministry with the Diocese of Llandaff in the deanery of Cardiff. He is also the author of several popular devotional books.

Life's Complicated: Pray Simply

The Reverend Andrew Highway

O&U
Onwards & Upwards

Onwards and Upwards Publishers
4 The Old Smithy
London Road
Rockbeare
EX5 2EA
United Kingdom

www.onwardsandupwards.org

First United States edition published by Hope & Life Press (2017).

First United Kingdom edition published by Onwards and Upwards Publishers Ltd. (2022).

ISBN: 978-1-78815-977-7
Typeface: Sabon LT

For Sarah, Isabelle, James and Georgina.

Contents

Contents (continued)

Introduction

How did life get this complicated? Despite all the advances in technology in our age, the sad fact is that for many of us our lives are now busier and more stressful than ever before. Just keeping up with the pace of postmodern, post-Christian life is exhausting as we are constantly told to keep moving, both physically and mentally. Unconsciously, we are haunted by a fear that if we stop, even for just a moment, we will be left behind, never to recover our place in the race of life. The pressure of living this way means that we never find the time for the things we really want to do: those things we know deep down really matter; the big stuff – life, the universe and God.

Making some space to think about God can appear daunting, and if we were to take it a little further and consider getting to a place where we would be ready to talk to God, to actually pray, how long would it take us to reach that point? Weeks, months, years? It is not just our perceived lack of time that stops us from starting to pray. Often it is a fear of how to pray and what to pray about that prevents us from entering into what for many seems to be this strange other world. There is often a misconception that prayer is complicated and that to pray in an effective way, long theological words need to be used to 'guarantee' success. But that is neither the way Jesus Christ, the only-begotten Son of God, Himself prayed, nor the way He taught people to pray. When Jesus prayed, He used language that was often simple, honest and reassuringly straightforward – prayer from the heart.

Knowing this, we can start to look at what prayer is in a different way. We can also start to understand that the prayers God wants to hear us pray are those that are simple and honest, from the depths of our hearts. Our prayers should be about the things that really bother us, the ordinary things: for example, how we feel; what we see; our experiences, fears and worries; our hopes, joys and aspirations. The list is endless, as God is interested in every aspect of our lives.

In short, we can pray about anything and everything that happens in our lives, which is why this small book is titled *Life's Complicated: Pray Simply.* At its heart, prayer is just a conversation with God, and to begin to pray, we just need to reach out in faith with words that are ordinary.

Pray Simply About Ordinary Things

"Pray continually."

1 Thessalonians 5:17

How can we pray at all times and in all places? Surely, that is the preserve of saints and deeply religious people, many think; not normal people like you and I. But if we were to embrace the idea of continually praying, praying without cease as the Apostle Paul said, then we would have to seriously reconsider what prayer is and the subjects we can pray about.

Thinking about prayer as being something that can happen anywhere, at any time, takes us away from a structured and formal idea of prayer, opening up a host of new possibilities. To appreciate prayer in this way lets us bring before God the ordinary things of our daily life. In turn, this allows the idea of praying continually to take on a new and more attainable meaning.

In this section, there are some very simple prayers about everyday things such as the commute to work, our local town centre, the coffee shop we frequent and the friends we meet. When we pray continually, it is because we are able to perceive God in all aspects of our life.

Twenty-Four Hours

O Lord,
let me be abandoned to Your will,
safe in the knowledge that You are my God.

Each morning when I wake,
give me a sense of Your purpose;
each day I live,
give me a desire to serve You;
each night I sleep,
give me rest in Your presence.
Forgive the distractions that cloud my soul,
make me open to Your ways, for You are my God.

Amen.

HOME

Heavenly Father, bless our home.

May it be a place of shelter
and safety in this troubled world;
may a sense of Your presence abide in it always;
may all who enter find rest
and peace within its walls.

May Your angels protect it
each day and each night, I pray,
in the name of the Father and of the Son
and of the Holy Spirit. †

Amen.

The Commute

Lord, this morning I hold before You those making their way to work, and as they travel, grant them safe passage to their destination.

Today, amidst the business of the world, make us vulnerable to Your love and let its power change and transform our broken lives.

Amen.

The Puncture

Ever-loving God, our lives often become like a punctured tyre – flat, worn – and lived out of alignment with You. When we are deflated by the disappointments of life, fill us with the peace, joy and love of the Holy Spirit.

When we become worn out on this relentless and emotional journey, renew us for the road ahead. When we realise our lives are out of alignment with Your will and purpose, help us realign ourselves with You. Equip us each day as we travel the appointed distance of our lives.

Amen.

A Smile

Lord,
I pray that today,
through an act of kindness
or a moment of selfless giving,
I may bring a smile to someone's face.

Amen.

Work

O Lord,
be with me in my work today.

When the task is mundane, make me joyful;
when I am granted success, make me thankful.

In all I do, keep my heart pure,
my mind focused and my words holy.

Amen.

The Working Week

Forgive me, Lord, that I saw Monday
as just a day to be ticked off.

Forgive me, Lord, that Tuesday was just to be got through
and that Wednesday was a mountain I had to climb.

Forgive me, Lord, that as Thursday closed,
I whispered, *Nearly there...* and that Friday
was the day I wished away.

Help me, Lord, to see my working week
as days that should be lived, cherished and valued.

May I greet each new morning with a prayer of thanks
and close each night with a prayer of praise.

Amen.

My Computer Prayer

Lord,

Make me wise in what I download,
what I listen to and what I watch;
always mindful that my life is
lived before You.

Amen.

Reminder – 9:55 Hours

(Pre-Meeting Prayer)

Lord,
in this meeting may I
listen with respect,
speak with wisdom,
act with integrity.

Prevent my mind from being distracted
and give me the strength to resist
the urge to check my phone.

Keep me attentive and focused
so that I might successfully
accomplish the task in hand.

Amen.

Retirement

Lord,
bless me in my retirement;
I pray that my days will be filled
with a sense of Your divine purpose.

Let me live always in the hope
and assurance of my faith;
give me opportunities to share
my experience and wisdom,
and make me conscious of using my time well,
being willing to give and ready to receive.

May my heart be filled
with contentment, happiness and joy;
I offer You this prayer
in the name of my Saviour, Jesus Christ.

Amen.

Reluctant Traveller

Lord Jesus Christ,
I am a reluctant traveller;
I fear the unexpected and
I miss the security of my home.

On this journey, provide the sense of peace
and assurance I need to enjoy my travels.

May I use the insecurity I feel
to give you thanks for all that I sometimes take for granted.
Bring me home safely.

Stay with me in all things.
And guide me through all things.

Amen.

Town Centre Prayer

Almighty, ever-present God,
we pray for our town centre in these times of change;
for the people who work in its shops,
give them peace in uncertainty.

For anyone who has recently lost their job,
give them hope for the future;
and for those whose decisions affect the town,
give them wisdom and discernment.

Surround our town and its people with your love,
and let us know your presence each day;
we ask these prayers
through our Lord Jesus Christ.

Amen.

The City

God,
thank You for the city, where people meet,
collide, exist and survive.

A place where buildings cohabit to bridge the gap of time;
clock towers and churches mix
with glass offices of corporate endeavour.

An urban space bursting with energy and purpose,
alive to the possibility and excitement of life;
where phones and lattes disconnect us
from the spiritual realm.

God, walk among us in our greed and consumerism;
teach us to see the marginalised, remember the forgotten,
reach out to the lonely.

We pray today for the city:
office, shop, club, home.

Amen.

The Shopping Centre

Lord God,
in this vast retail cathedral,
I feel disconnected from Your presence;
my senses are bombarded by designer labels and global brands;
I am a consumer lost in a world of materialism.

Provide me with the strength to distinguish
between the superficial wealth of this world
and Your gift of eternal life
offered through Jesus Christ.

Amen.

The Eye Test

Lord,
thank you for my optician's appointment today.

Thank you for my eye test,
thank you for my new glasses,
thank you for the skill of the optician.

I pray that each morning when I open my eyes,
I may have a renewed sense of wonder at the world I see;
its colours, shapes and images.

May I never take for granted
the gift of sight that You give me.

Amen.

Enough

Oh, Lord,
have we lost the concept
of what it is to have enough?

Are we simply consumers,
manipulated into feeling dissatisfied?

How many clothes do we need to own
before we have enough?
When does the supermarket trolley
finally contain enough?

At what point do our possessions
ever become enough?

Holy Spirit, give us each the wisdom
to recognise that we have too much,
rather than not enough.

Amen.

Contentment

Lord,
I thank You that each day
You provide for my needs.

Make me satisfied with all I have
and keep my heart from craving material things.

May my heart's desire be for Your love,
which is eternal;
a love freely given
and that I may freely receive.

Amen.

Declutter

Lord Jesus,
guard me from the accumulation
of possessions.

Give me the strength and wisdom
to regularly declutter my life
from the material things that weigh me down.

Let me realise that my value as a person
is not measured in the things I own,
but in what I say and do.

Renew in me a focus to be emptied of the need to have
and filled with a desire to give.

Amen.

A Coffee Shop Prayer

Lord, I pray for the people
in this coffee shop:
the staff who are employed, grant them patience
and a smile as they work.

The mother with her baby, grant them both protection
from the evils of this world;
the businessman sitting alone,
grant him a safe journey home tonight.

The school children, full of life,
grant them wise decisions in the years to come;
the young couple so much in love,
grant them joy in the time they spend together.

I hold before You all these people,
for they are Yours;
You made them in Your own image
and You love them.

Amen.

A Patient's Prayer

Grant unto me, O Lord,
peace when I am fearful,
healing in my pain
and hope when I despair.

Enfold me in Your eternal love,
I pray.

Amen.

The Hospital

Lord Jesus,
make our churches hospitals for wounded souls;
let them be places that care
for those who have been hurt by life.

Fill us with compassion to help,
make broken people whole again,
and teach us to love
without judgement or prejudice.

Jesus, our Healer,
through Your resurrection power,
restore each one of us
so we can live our days
filled with the Holy Spirit.

Amen.

LONELINESS

Today
I am lonely.

Wandering around the playground
without a friend;
struggling to find my place
in a teenage world.

Trapped in the house
with two small children;
travelling on business
away from my family.

Lying in hospital
afraid of the future;
sitting in my chair
hoping someone will call.

O Lord, You said
it is not good for man to live alone,[1]
so today, I pray for:

light in the darkness,
hope in despair
and presence in solitude.

Amen.

[1] Genesis 2:18

A Memory Prayer

Lord,
today, I forgot the things
I should have remembered.

In these moments,
help me in my fear and frustration
to rest in the assurance
that You will never forget me.

Amen.

FRIENDS

Lord,
I thank You for my friends.

For all we have shared together,
the times of laughter and tears;
joy and pain,
hope and despair.

Thank You that they forgive my failings
and rejoice in my success;
thank You for their friendship
and support.

Amen.

Loss

Lord,
why did this happen?
Can't you hear the cries
of my broken heart?

I know this baby could have
done great things for You;
now, I am just numb.

The blackness surrounds, engulfs,
and consumes my world;
please give me strength
to bear this loss.

Into Your hands I place
my future hopes and fears;
hold me
with Your steadfast love.

Amen.

Faithful Friend

Lord Jesus,
thank You for our pet *[name]*,
a faithful friend.

Thank You for all the joy s/he gave us,
for the happy memories we will always treasure,
for the love and affection s/he so freely gave us.

Lord,
please give us strength at this sad time
as we say goodbye;
we thank you for the gift
of *[name]* in our lives.

Amen.

Success

Lord God,
in a world that celebrates the success,
celebrity and achievement of a few,
teach us to recognise and value
the gifts and talents of all Your people.

Amen.

Life

Lord Jesus,
when I am afraid, strengthen me;
when I am discouraged,
empower me.

When I feel abandoned,
reassure me;
when I feel alone,
console me.

In all places and at all times,
be near me, I pray.

Amen.

HIRAETH[2]

God, our Protector;
God, our Provider;
God, our Healer.

Praise You for our place
of rest and calm – *hiraeth.*

Praise You for our constant
in a changing world – *hiraeth.*

Praise You for our refuge
in the raging storm – *hiraeth.*

Praise You for our home,
where love abides,
hope is nurtured
and joy abounds – *hiraeth.*

Amen.

[2] *Hiraeth* is a Welsh word with no direct English translation. It is often used in the Welsh language to refer to a longing or yearning

Pray Simply When Seeking God

"For whoever finds Me finds life."

Proverbs 8:35

The word 'spirituality' is often used to describe the search or quest of a person for God. When we come as ordinary people before an extraordinary God, we do so praying simply, honestly, and with humility. An important part of seeking God is self-examination: when we look at ourselves and assess how far away or how near we are to God. As part of this process, we may consider the things that stand between God and us, and how He may be drawing near to us in different ways. We may also reflect on some areas of our lives to which we need to pay particular attention.

The prayers in this section are about spirituality and the whole process of seeking God. It is recognised that each person will do this in a different way, so these simple prayers are starting points and not destinations in themselves. Thinking about who we really are and at what place in our lives we are, helps us to be open to the possibilities God has for our lives.

My Life

Dear Lord,
I look back on my life and I realise
that I have lived each day
in the years that have passed.

Some days have been filled with joy and laughter,
others with pain and tears;
but today I realise
that I have lived each one.

Some days, I have given to You
and lived for Your glory;
and other days,
I wasted on selfish ambition.

Help me to cherish each day:
not to rush, but to pause;
help me to seek Your will
each and every day.

Above all,
help me to live for You.

Amen.

Random

Lord,
I don't believe my life
exists as a set of random circumstances;
I don't believe my life
consists of a set of coincidences.[3]

I believe You are a God
who guides my steps each day;
I believe You are a God
who has a divine plan and purpose for my life.

Lord,
give me the faith to trust
that Your ways may not always be my ways;
give me the strength to understand in all things
You are working for my good.

Amen.

[3] Based on Isaiah 55:9 / Romans 8:28

The Way

Lord,
we walk the way of our pilgrimage,
praying that this journey would change us from within;
as faithful pilgrims, heal our broken lives
by drawing us back to You.

As faithful pilgrims, teach us to live in the moment
by resting in the present;
as faithful pilgrims, may we learn to value
those we travel alongside.

As faithful pilgrims, awaken us to a deeper appreciation
of Your creation;
as faithful pilgrims, grant us strength
through Your Holy Spirit.

Lord,
bless us as we travel along the way;
grant us peace of mind,
body and spirit each day.

Amen.

To Follow

Lord Jesus Christ,
to follow You, I realise
that I must put aside my ambition,
my plans and my ego.

Make it my heart's desire
to know Your presence,
Your peace and Your purpose.

Amen.

A Simple Life

Lord,
make me content to live a simple life.

A life which is focused on You,
where the things I treasure
are only those of true value.

Where a love of people overcomes
my own pride, ego and agenda;
where I can balance the things I want
against the things I really need.

Bless me, Lord, as I strive
to live a peaceful, quiet, and holy life;
in the name of the Father,
the Son and the Holy Spirit.

Amen.

IDOLS

Lord,
turn our hearts
away from idols.

May our eyes be focused
on the one true God,
Maker of heaven and earth;
who stretched out His arms of love,
and whose Spirit dwells within us.

Amen.

A Thin Place

Almighty God,
let Your hand be on this place;
accept the prayers of Your people
poured out in praise.

Here the veil is slight,
between heaven's vast sky
and earth's tilled land;
this is a thin place,[4] O Lord.

Here You are the silence,
the stillness, that pervades my soul,
my rest and my peace.
This is a thin place, O Lord.

Here Your Spirit moves
across the contours of the land.
This is a thin place, O Lord.

Amen.

[4] *Thin Place* is a term often used in Celtic spirituality to refer to a place where it is perceived that the gap between heaven and earth is slight

The Second Chance

I have let others down,
I have let myself down;
Father, God,
I am so sorry.

Thank You that You forgive me,
love me and restore me;
today, I am a prodigal child running home
into the arms of my loving, heavenly Father.

Thank You that I am forgiven unconditionally,
thank You that I am loved eternally,
thank You that I am restored completely.

Thank You, Father, that You
are the God of second chances.

Amen.

Regret

O Lord,
on our earthly pilgrimage,
may we live our lives free of all regret.

Make us mindful of words
that may hurt another
and actions that cannot be undone.

Allow us to be open to new possibilities,
being conscious that fear of change
can shackle our faith.

At the close of the day,
save us from the regret of treasures
we have wasted or talents we have buried.

Amen.

Why

Loving, heavenly Father,
we pray for those who today ask, "Why?"

We pray for those who have questions
but can find no answers;
we pray for those who hear no words,
just an awkward silence.

Assure them that you are the God
who cares for the broken.
Assure them that you are the God
who heals the wounded.

Be near them each hour, each day
and each week that lies ahead.

Amen.

The Disappointment

I am disappointed because the situation did not work out as I had planned. Although words are hard, I can say that I trust You, God.[5]

I know You have a plan and a purpose for my life, and that You will work together all things for my good. Through the disappointment, I will keep praying, "I trust You, God."

Amen.

[5] Meditating on the promise of Romans 8:28

THE CROSSROADS

Lord,
I have reached a crossroads.[6]

Do I turn left?
Do I turn right?
Should I go back the way I have travelled
or should I continue into the unknown?

I look back at the landmarks of my faith,
prayers I have whispered,
prayers I have shouted;
silent prayers.

Each one a step of faith
on my journey with You;
every answer an assurance
of Your presence.

Lord,
show me the way to go;
be the light before me,
be the companion beside me.

Lord,
lead me to my place of rest and peace.

Amen.

[6] Meditation on Jeremiah 6:16.

CONFESSION

Almighty God,
in a moment of quietness,
I reflect on the day that has passed,
and humbly confess those things
for which I need Your forgiveness.

Amen.

Me

Lord,
may I rejoice
in the permission
to be me.

Me is the story of my past,
and the gift of my present.

It is the sum of both my strengths
and my weaknesses;
it encompasses all my hopes
and dreams.

Me is my story,
me is who I am.

Amen.

The Light

To those in our church who suffer pain:
Jesus, be the light in the darkness.

To those in our church who are alone:
Jesus, be the light in the darkness.

To those in our church who feel afraid:
Jesus, be the light in the darkness.

To those in our community who suffer injustice:
Jesus, be the light in the darkness.

To those in our community who are marginalised:
Jesus, be the light in the darkness.

To those in our community who feel abandoned:
Jesus, be the light in the darkness.

To those in our world who suffer poverty:
Jesus, be the light in the darkness.

To those in our world who are at risk of disease:
Jesus, be the light in the darkness.

To those in our world who feel threatened by violence:
Jesus, be the light in the darkness.

Amen.

Waiting

O Lord,
I wait for You;
show me Your ways.

Reveal the next step I should take,
inform the choices that I make,
guide me by Your Holy Spirit, I pray.

In the stillness of waiting,
grant me wisdom,
patience and discernment.

Amen.

The Retreat

Awaken me to Your presence,
O God;
still my restless soul from the distractions
of the material world I inhabit.

May I search afresh for You,
inspired by the drama of Your creation;
uplift my soul with words of prayer
that declare Your glory.

Strengthen my resolve with a renewed love
and dependence on Your provision;
care for me and those I love
while I am on retreat.

Amen.

Vocation

Lord,
help me to discern my life's vocation;
to listen intently to Your voice,
and to be obedient to the call.

To fulfil this notion,
this prompting, this urge,
I want to serve You with all I have,
and offer You all that I can be.

Bless me in my vocation, I pray,
in the name of the Father,
and of the Son,
and of the Holy Spirit. †

Amen.

The Priest

How can I lead these people?
How can I love them when they hurt me?
How can I be worthy to stand at the altar?
How can I accept that I will make mistakes?

How can I say sorry when I am wrong?
How can I always find the right words to say?
How can I know when to be silent?
How can I be their priest?

Only through God's love,
Christ will work through me,
and the Holy Spirit dwell in me.

My call is to try, to fail,
to learn, to serve and to love;
make me worthy of my call.

Amen.

Awakening

From the trivial preoccupations of my life,
my heart is awakened to You, O Lord;
slowly I am drawn away from a random world
which consumes my time and energy.

In Your presence, I am still.
You are the eternal God,
changeless, personal and mysterious.

I yearn to deepen my experience of You
and fill the void in my soul with Your Spirit.
Dwell in me anew, O Lord.

Forgive me,
heal me,
know me.

Amen.

HOPE

At times of faith and doubt,
Lord Jesus, I place my hope in You;
when chaos brings uncertainty,
Lord Jesus, I place my hope in You.

In the anxiety of sickness,
Lord Jesus, I place my hope in You;
when caring seems a burden,
Lord Jesus, I place my hope in You.

In the pain of disappointment,
Lord Jesus, I place my hope in You;
for my eternal salvation,
Lord Jesus, I place my hope in You.

Amen.

Love

God,
Your love defies human understanding;
it is a love too deep
and mysterious to comprehend.

A love so powerful, it has the capacity
to forgive a past and define a future;
a love revealed in the atoning sacrifice
of Your Son, Jesus Christ.

A love surrounding the ordinary
moments of a busy day;
praise You, God, for Your love
which transcends all things!

Amen.

Praise

My heart overflows with praise
for my God.

The God of my youth,
the God of my middle years,
the God of my old age,
is the God of my eternity.

Amen.

KINDNESS

To be kind is to give
when we want to take;
to seek others when
we crave our own space.

To encourage when
we long to be inspired;
and to do when
our urge is to rest.

Lord,
ingrain in us Your spirit of kindness
which transcends our feelings,
moods and emotions.

Amen.

Creative Lives

Creator God,
inspire us to live creative lives,
where the things we write, make and say
are true expressions of ourselves that enhance,
rather than diminish, the value of Your world.

Amen.

The Dawn

Lord Jesus,
lead me out of the darkness
into Your light.

Be my consolation in times of despair
and deliver me to a place of inner peace;
walk alongside me when the path is too steep
and guide me when I am lost.

In the pain of today, assure me
that there is hope for tomorrow;
by faith, I will wait for the night to pass
and for the dawn to arrive.

Amen.

Contemplation

God,
You lie beyond my intellect and emotion,
and yet are always present.

In my prayer, turn my restless body to stillness;
let my words fall into silence
and dispel my distracting thoughts.

Through the surrender of my will,
may I become open to Your possibilities.

Amen.

THIS MUCH

Lord,
how much do You love me?

...†his much.

Thank You,
Lord Jesus,
for the Cross.

Amen.

The Good Shepherd

Lord, Jesus Christ,
You are the good shepherd
and we are Your sheep.
When we are lost,
You find us and lead us home.[7]

When we are wounded and hurt,
You carry us home;
when we stray from the right path,
Your voice calls us home.

Thank You,
Lord Jesus,
that You are the good shepherd
who lays down His life for His sheep.

Amen.

[7] John 10:11

Pray Simply Through the Year

"There is a time for everything and a season
for every activity under heaven."

Ecclesiastes 3:1

The calendar of the Church has seasons, just like the one that hangs on your kitchen wall. These give the Christian year a rhythm all of its own.

Starting in December, the calendar begins with Advent and the expectation of the birth of our Saviour, Jesus Christ. Then it moves to the joy of Christmas. As we enter the first throws of spring, we then pause for 40 days. This is called Lent. It is a time when we have the chance to reflect and think about our relationship with God, before we enter into the sorrow of Holy Week and the glory of the resurrection of Christ on Easter Day. The rest of the year is just called Ordinary Time.

It is ironic that much of the Christian year is seen as being rather mundane, perhaps because aside from the great festivals of Christmas and Easter, the life of the Christian is about ordinary things and how we cope with them, which in turn should shape the way we pray. The prayers in this section help us to reflect on some significant dates in the Church calendar. These key events act as way markers that can guide us as we journey through life across the landscape of the seasons.

The Church

Lord Jesus,
hear my prayer in this sacred place;
close my mind to the pressures of the world outside,
open my heart to the sense of Your presence.

In this silence, grant me rest;
in this stillness, give me peace;
in this moment, restore my hope;
as I leave this church, let me know that I am
surrounded by Your love.

Give me a peace in my heart
that the world cannot give;[8]
bless me, Lord,
(† The sign of the cross may be made)
in the name of the Father
and of the Son
and of the Holy Spirit.

Amen.

[8] Jn 14:27

People of God

Loving and merciful Father,
we come before You
gathered together as Your people.

Grant our hearts and minds stillness before You,
O Lord;
to You be all glory and praise.

Accept our thanks for all that we have;
we offer up our lives to You,
all we are and all we can be.

Equip us each day
with Your Holy Spirit;
make us faithful witnesses.

Make us humble servants,
make us worthy ambassadors,
make us truly the people of God.

Amen.

Advent

Almighty God,
this Advent, we prepare to celebrate the birth
of our Saviour, Jesus Christ.

Grant us the courage to turn our attention
away from the pressures of this world;
grant us the strength to call to mind those things
for which we need Your forgiveness.

This season, restore in our hearts
Your eternal peace, that we may find happiness,
contentment and fulfilment
in a life lived with You.

Amen.

Ash Wednesday

Almighty God,
today I want to put aside the things
I have built around me to help me cope.

I want to focus on You and recover
my commitment to be Your disciple;
I want to follow You more truly and be
more faithful in thought, action and prayer.

I want to use this Lent to restore
my sense of communion with You.
(Bow head / Pause / † Sign of the cross)

In the name of the Father
and of the Son
and of the Holy Spirit.

Amen.

Lent

Lord Jesus Christ,
cleanse my mind, body and spirit
from the things that clutter my life;
drive out my ego, my ambition
and my need to be in control.

Make my body a temple where
the Holy Spirit can dwell;
help me to create space in my life
for worship, prayer and thanksgiving.

Amen.

Maundy Thursday

Lord Jesus,
tonight, I remember:
those times when I have denied You,
forgive me, Lord;
those times when I have lived for myself,
forgive me, Lord;
those times when I watched as others mocked You,
forgive me, Lord;
those times when I have run away in fear,
forgive me, Lord.

Lord Jesus, I love You,
heal me;
Lord Jesus, I love You,
strengthen me;
Lord Jesus, I love You,
restore me.

Amen.

Trinity

Everlasting God:
our Creator,
our Redeemer,
our Breath.

One God,
Father, Son and Holy Spirit.
†

Amen.

Harvest

Creator God,
we praise You for Your faithful
and generous provision of the harvest;
we thank You for the changing seasons
which nourished and sustained the earth this year.

We ask Your blessing upon the farmers
who work the land to grow the crops,
and for those employed in the production
and sale of our daily bread.

Give us compassionate hearts
toward those who are hungry,
so that in our abundance,
we may meet their need.

Accept this offering
of our harvest to You,
O God.

Amen.

Christ the King

We praise You,
Lord Jesus Christ.

You walked among us
in Galilee,
You taught and healed.

You died among us
on Calvary,
in pain and sorrow.

You reign victorious
in Heaven,
the Alpha and the Omega.[9]

Amen.

[9] Revelation 22:13

EVENSONG

Lord,
in the stillness of the evening,
we lift our eyes to You.

Watch over us this night.

We give You all that happened to us,
the things achieved
and the mistakes made.

Guard our hearts and minds as we sleep;
grant us Your peace in our rest.

Amen.

MARRIAGE

Almighty God,
bless our marriage this day,
we ask;
may we always seek to afford one another
our complete love, trust and respect.

As the years unfold,
grant us the grace to celebrate
each other's successes,
and the ability to bear together
life's disappointments.

Make our home a place of sanctuary
that provides a refuge from the world outside;
fill our lives with your love, and grant us the strength
to remain faithful to those promises
which we have made today.

We ask our prayer in Your name.

Amen.

Child's Blessing

[Name], in your life ahead
there are so many choices to make
and so much to experience and see.

I pray that each day you will seek God's blessing,
ask for His guidance
and depend upon His wisdom.

Amen.

A Candle Prayer

(A Candle is Lit)

Lord Jesus Christ,
You are the light of the world[10]
who shines in the darkness;
the One whom the darkness
will not overcome.

Hear my prayer.

Amen.

[10] Based on John 1:5

A Vestry Prayer[11]

God, our Saviour,
in this our time of worship
may our intention be to glorify You;
may our words reflect Your majesty
and may our actions submit to Your authority.

We ask our prayer
through Jesus Christ, our Lord.

Amen.

[11] Based on Jude :25

A Prayer for Holocaust Memorial Day

Lord God of Abraham, Isaac and Jacob,
today we commemorate
Holocaust Memorial Day.

We remember each name
that was a life cut short,
and each face
that became a number.

In the place of execution
there remains a silence
and the unanswerable question:
Why?

But our hope remains
in a love
that sets us free.

Amen.

Pray Simply in the World

"The Lord is my shepherd, I shall not be in want.
He makes me lie down in green pastures,
He leads me beside still waters,
He restores my soul."

Psalm 23:1-3

These verses are very familiar and come from one of the best-loved of all the psalms in the Bible. Written by David, who was a great king of Israel, they draw on his own experience as a young shepherd boy taking care of his family's flocks on the deserted hillsides around Bethlehem. The time David spent in those remote places led him to understand how he could find God all around him, in the world in which he lived. David saw God as the Shepherd who could lead him to green pastures and still waters in the time of his distress, just as he himself had cared for the sheep when still a shepherd. In this beautiful psalm, David teaches us to find God in the world in which we live; a world we know best.

This last section of prayers shows how we can still find God in our postmodern world. Sometimes, we can use our own experience of the natural world to form a simple prayer, but often it is in and from the ordinary that we can get our inspiration. Even wind turbines and lifeboats can be subjects of prayer. Just like David, we are asking God to lead us to places that restore our souls, after they have been battered and bruised by a busy world.

THE ESCAPE

Thank You, Lord,
for the silence
to think, to walk,
to pray, to be.

Amen.

MORNING

Lord,
in the morning, I worship You
for the sun that is yet to rise,
for the day that is yet to live.

You are my God,
my Lord,
my Saviour;
walk with me this day.

Amen.

A Walk

Praise God for my lunchtime walk,
a full thirty minutes immersed in another world;
praise God that my polished shoes tread under
a canopy of trees instead of rows of fluorescent lights.

Praise God that my eyes are filled with nature's beauty
instead of a screen full of emails;
praise God for the woodpecker in the branches,
the newts in the pond and the squirrel crossing my path.

Praise God that my familiar office is replaced
by sights and sounds that make me
an insecure stranger.

Praise God that a place once polluted by man
is now restored by the hand
of its Creator.

Amen.

The Garden

Creator God,
praise You for the garden that
each season is renewed by Your hand.

Praise You for the birds that forage
in the winter snows;
praise You for the first blooms
drenched by the spring rains.

Praise You for the long and lazy days
under the summer sun;
praise You for the golden leaves
falling in the autumn winds.

Creator God,
thank You for the sounds,
scents and colours
of my garden.

Amen.

March Wind

Lord,
praise You for the arrival of the March wind
that blows away my winter gloom;
praise You for the sun that gently warms my face
and instantly lifts my spirit.

Praise You for the chattering birdsong that demands
I must stop and listen;
praise You for the return of the vast blue skies
with their trails of dancing clouds.

These signs herald the arrival of spring
and remind me to look for the invisible God
in the hidden moments of each day.

Amen.

August

God,
in the midst of an urban sprawl,
I find myself chasing after
the silence of Your presence.

I need to disconnect
from my chaotic world,
and pursue a peace
that transcends my understanding.[12]

Beneath an August sky,
surrounded by sculptured trees,
I begin to reconnect
with the living God.

Amen.

[12] Philippians 4:7

The Sea View

Lord,
thank You for the view
outside my window.

Praise You for the endless sky,
vast and ever-changing;
praise You for the rolling patchwork
of bleached brown hills.

Praise You for the grazing cattle,
specks in a distant pasture;
praise You for the granite church,
weathered, but reassuring.

Praise You for the gulls that swoop
and turn to catch the breeze;
praise You for the rows of coloured houses
squinting in the sun.

Praise You for the emerald tide
which ebbs and flows each day.
For all I see, for all I hear,
for all I sense, thank You.

Amen.

THE VILLAGE

Thank You, Lord,
for the village that lies before me;
nestling in a wooded dell,
its luminous stone weathered
by each passing season.

A place where the soundtrack to the day
is not voices, music or traffic,
but birdsong from the treetops.

This morning, I am grateful
that people still smile
and know my name.

For the shop selling everything I need
and nothing I want;
for the memorial garden
bearing the names of the fallen.

For the parish church,
a timeless place of quiet prayer;
and for the stream with its fish
chasing the gentle current.

Thank You, Lord,
for the village.

Amen.

The Lifeboat

Almighty God,
we pray for our lifeboat crew;
protect them as they sail to help
those who are in distress.

Grant them wisdom
in the duties they perform,
and sustain them
through the trials they face.

Be near those who wait behind,
assure them of Your presence
and calm their fears.

Watch over the boat
and, this day / night,
bring her crew safely home.

Amen.

The Wind Turbine

The bright white wind turbine
looks ugly perched high
on the sandstone hill.

Its steel blades endlessly turned
by an invisible force;
a giant mechanical daffodil
stealing wind from the chasing clouds.

Who's to blame for this scar on the rural landscape?
The energy provider for generating
a greener, more sustainable power?

The farmer for adapting the land
to meet a commercial need?
Or is it me, with my insatiable demand
for electricity to power my modern life?

Lord,
forgive my speed to judge
and my unwillingness to see
the consequence of the way I live,
to the beauty of your creation.

Amen.

Stepping Stones

Lord,
help us to make time
to meet You
throughout our day.

Teach us to pause
in the moment
and learn to dwell
in Your presence.

Awaken our spirits
to the wonder of nature,
leading us to praise You,
its Creator.

Let us ponder with honesty
how to make
our lives more relevant
to our faith.

May our encounters
with You each day
be stepping stones
along our earthly journey.

Amen.

LANDSCAPE

Creator God,
Your presence
pervades my senses.

Stretching before me
is a landscape of arid beauty,
framed by dry stone walls.

Birdsong echoes
from a distant copse,
carried on a languid wind.

Ever-present God,
in this moment,
I praise You
for all that lies before me.

Amen.

Night

Lord,
protect me through this night,
I pray.

Let my mind find peace,
and my body find rest;
guard me with Your angels
as I sleep.

(† Sign of the Cross may be made)

Amen.

A Rainbow

Loving God,
I believe You always send
a rainbow after the rain;
each colour a reminder
of a different aspect of Your love:

Red – compassionate
Orange – eternal
Yellow – faithful
Green – unchanging
Blue – steadfast
Indigo – unconditional
Violet – forgiving.

A rainbow
is a promise
to me
of Your love.

Amen.

BLESSING

May you live
in the light of God's
abundant love,
and the expectation
of His eternity.

Amen.

Similar Books from the Publisher

A Pocketful of Prayers

Joan Copeland

ISBN 978-1-910197-18-9

This booklet contains 28 prayers in the form of poems that cover aspects of life that we all face – from birthdays to Christmas, from trust to forgiveness, from remembering the past to expectancy of the future.

In Short

Sue O'Donnell

ISBN 978-1-907509-66-7

This heart-warming devotional was birthed out of Sue O'Donnell's daily journey with the Lord. Perfect for daily readings and quiet meditation, these morsels of wisdom and worship will inspire and grow your own personal relationship with Jesus.

Books available from all good bookshops and from the publisher: **www.onwardsandupwards.org**